HELL'S CANYON
BY EMILY SHEEHAN

CURRENCY PRESS
SYDNEY

✛ LA MAMA

THE OLD
505
THEATRE

CURRENT THEATRE SERIES

First published in 2018
by Currency Press Pty Ltd,
PO Box 2287, Strawberry Hills, NSW, 2012, Australia
enquiries@currency.com.au
www.currency.com.au

Typeset by Dean Nottle for Currency Press.
Cover image by Ellen Stanistreet. Cover design by Jen Tran.
Cover shows Isabelle Ford and Conor Leach.

A catalogue record for this
book is available from the
National Library of Australia

NATIONAL
LIBRARY
OF AUSTRALIA

Contents

Currency Press acknowledges the Traditional Owners of the Country on which we live and work. We pay our respects to all Aboriginal and Torres Strait Islander Elders, past and present.

For Tomas,
who raged against the world with me
when I was seventeen.

Hell's Canyon was first presented at The Old 505 Theatre, Sydney, on 1 August 2018 and transferred to La Mama Theatre, Melbourne, on 12 September 2018, with the following cast:

CAITLIN	Isabelle Ford
OSCAR	Conor Leach

Director, Katie Cawthorne
Designer, Tyler Ray Hawkins
Sound Designer, Kimmo Vennonen
Stage Manager, Laura Barnes

The play was developed with Playwriting Australia at the National Script Workshop and the National Play Festival.

CHARACTERS

CAITLIN, 17, wears a hoodie, denim skirt and high-tops

OSCAR, 15, wears a baggy polo shirt with a school logo, cargo
    shorts and dirty sneakers

SETTING

Scene One: a public park
Scene Two: a motel room

PUNCTUATION

/   indicates the exact point of interruption in overlapping dialogue

…   indicates the character is choosing not to speak

This play went to press before the end of rehearsals and may differ
from the play as performed.

SCENE ONE

A public park. Red brick wall. Cement. A green wheelie bin. A rusty swing that could give you tetanus.

CAITLIN *swings on the swing.* OSCAR *catches his breath.*

CAITLIN: Twelve past three, I'm impressed.
OSCAR: Came straight from school.
CAITLIN: Musta run.
OSCAR: …
CAITLIN: …
OSCAR: You look nice. I like your … hoodie.
CAITLIN: Do I look hot?
OSCAR: Um, you look like Caitlin.
CAITLIN: Wanna go skinny dipping in the river?
OSCAR: You mean without clothes on?
CAITLIN: Dare me?
OSCAR: Is this a prank?
CAITLIN: I will if you will.
OSCAR: Naked?
CAITLIN: Yep.
OSCAR: Butt naked?
CAITLIN: Pants off, dick out, naked.
OSCAR: In public?
CAITLIN: No-one'll see, no-one comes here.
OSCAR: *You'll* see.
CAITLIN: You afraid?
OSCAR: How 'bout top half only?
CAITLIN: That's obviously unfair.
OSCAR: I dunno …
CAITLIN: I'll go anyway. I don't care.
OSCAR: What if there's crocs?
CAITLIN: No way, that's way further downstream.
OSCAR: Better not.
CAITLIN: I'm gonna risk it. You coming?

OSCAR: Why're we even here?

CAITLIN: You wanna make out?

OSCAR: Your text was legit?

CAITLIN: What do you think?

OSCAR *takes out his phone.*

OSCAR: [*reading the text message*] 'Oscar. Full stop. Wanna fuck. Question mark. Maluka Park. Full stop.'

CAITLIN: Cryptic huh?

OSCAR: You're messing, right?

CAITLIN: I thought I was pretty straightforward.

OSCAR: Promise this isn't some awful prank where you'll take a photo of me and send it round school—

CAITLIN: I literally never even considered that.

OSCAR: —and come up with some whip-smart caption that someone turns into a meme and I'm left immortalised online but for all the wrong reasons.

CAITLIN: That does sound like me, doesn't it?

OSCAR: Because yeah, you're not the nicest person of all time, but that would be like on another level.

CAITLIN: It's not a prank.

OSCAR: …

CAITLIN: I'm game if you are.

OSCAR: For real?

CAITLIN: For real.

OSCAR: Yeah alright.

They start to make out. Furious. Sloppy. Uncoordinated.

Wait! Stop. No.

This is the most awkward thing of my life.

I'm just gonna leave.

CAITLIN: What?

OSCAR: Cya round.

CAITLIN: You're lucky to even be here, you know that?

OSCAR: Don't be mad, I feel guilty.

CAITLIN: You're such a joke.

OSCAR: I said I'm sorry. I'm just *thrown.*

CAITLIN: You *ran* here.

OSCAR: I didn't run, it was more like a fast walk if you wanna get technical.

CAITLIN: You clearly ran, you're all sweaty.

OSCAR: I'll have you know I'm always sweaty.

CAITLIN: It's called antiperspirant.

OSCAR: It's called anti-what-the-heck-I-don't-wanna-do-it-with-you.

CAITLIN: Then why'd you even come, I coulda texted someone else if you were gonna wimp out.

OSCAR: I was happy you were talkin' t' me for the first time in like six months. I thought you'd have some sorta speech prepared.

CAITLIN: You isolated yourself, Oscar. I just went along with it.

OSCAR: Is that your version of an apology?

Silence.

CAITLIN: Let's do something fun.

OSCAR: I should probably go home.

CAITLIN: You're so boring.

OSCAR: It's mocks tomorrow. Not that you'd know, you haven't been at school.

CAITLIN: Yeah yeah.

OSCAR: Haven't seen you there in ages.

CAITLIN: What's your point?

OSCAR: You're gonna get so thick you'll have to repeat Year Ten. Then you'll be in my class.

CAITLIN: You mean the spaz class?

OSCAR: Don't worry, I'll let you copy my homework.

CAITLIN: Then I'll definitely be put in the spaz class if I'm copying off you.

OSCAR: You shouldn't use the word 'spaz'.

CAITLIN: You shouldn't care so much about mocks, it's not like it's the actual exams.

OSCAR: I want to do well.

CAITLIN: You'll be fine, you're like a child genius.

C'mon, Os.

Hey, wanna know a secret?

OSCAR: No.

…

Okay yes, I obviously do. What? Tell me.

CAITLIN: Wanna see my tattoo?

OSCAR: You don't have a tattoo.

CAITLIN: I do now.

OSCAR: I know that you don't.

CAITLIN: You don't know shit.

OSCAR: I assume that you don't.

CAITLIN: I assume your tighty whities have skid marks fifty percent of the time, give or take.

OSCAR: … You can't get a tattoo if you're under eighteen.

CAITLIN: Yes you can.

OSCAR: Not without permission, and your mum's way strict.

CAITLIN: You can if you suck off the guy at the parlour.

OSCAR: … You're a psycho.

…

So can I see your tattoo?

CAITLIN: Nup, missed your chance.

OSCAR: I knew you were lying.

> CAITLIN *sits next to* OSCAR, *checks no-one's looking. Shimmies up her skirt.*

[*Shielding his eyes*] Ahhhh, my eyes!

CAITLIN: Hey.

OSCAR: Just kidding. Show me.

> CAITLIN *shimmies up her skirt. Above her knee a sheet of plastic is wrapped around her thigh. She peels it back to reveal a large tattoo of a spiny flower with purple leaves. Below the tattoo, her leg is visibly bruised. Along the length of her knee is a deep gash that has recently been stitched up.*

CAITLIN: Cool, hey?

OSCAR: It's all oozy.

CAITLIN: It'll look different in a month. When the swelling and scabs go away.

OSCAR: Can I touch it?

CAITLIN: Go ahead.

> OSCAR *traces the tattoo gently, then moves to touch the stitches.*

[*Flinching*] Ouch.

OSCAR: Still hurts?

CAITLIN: Colours are more intense than black ink.

OSCAR: What is it?

CAITLIN: Deadly nightshade. One of the most poisonous plants ever. Eating the berries makes you hallucinate … if you're lucky.

OSCAR: What if you're unlucky?

CAITLIN: [*miming slitting her throat*] Kkkkkkkk!

OSCAR: Woah.

CAITLIN: I'm the only girl at school with a tattoo. So that's pretty cool. Bet everyone will copy now. You wanna get one? I can take you.

OSCAR: No way.

CAITLIN: C'mon, it'll be fun.

OSCAR: There's nothing fun about terrible, irreversible decisions.

CAITLIN: It wasn't a terrible decision.

OSCAR: You'll regret it tomorrow.

CAITLIN: Shut the fuck up, Oscar.

OSCAR: I mean, if going the flower route wasn't a lame cliché, giving gobbies to tattoo artists is probably on your list of Top Five Trashiest Moments.

CAITLIN: Shut up, you dipshit! You don't know fucking anything about why I did it, so don't try to be cool, okay!

OSCAR: Hey, are you okay?

CAITLIN: Yes I'm fine.

OSCAR: Are you sad because you're already regretting it?

CAITLIN: I don't need you being a dickhead to me right now, okay, because I've actually had a really, really terrible day.

OSCAR: How bad?

CAITLIN: Really bad.

OSCAR: Worse than Kanye?

CAITLIN: Way worse than Kanye.

OSCAR: Yikes. Wanna talk about it?

CAITLIN: No I don't wanna talk to you about it. I have way, *way* better friends I would talk to before you.

OSCAR: When I'm feeling down, it's usually because—

CAITLIN: I said shut up, Oscar. This is why you don't have any friends.

Pause. They sit in an awkward silence.

OSCAR slowly takes a sandwich wrapped in aluminum foil out of his backpack. He unwraps it slowly. It's extremely noisy and irritates CAITLIN.

OSCAR: [*chewing*] Wanna bite? Ham and cheese.

CAITLIN: Fat chicks and five-year-olds eat ham and cheese.

OSCAR: I like ham and cheese—

CAITLIN: So what does that make you?

OSCAR: That's a bit reductive—

CAITLIN: Your brain's a bit reductive—

OSCAR: Your brain's a bit destructive—

CAITLIN: That doesn't even make sense—

OSCAR: You don't even make sense—

CAITLIN: Alright stop—

OSCAR: Collaborate and listen.

OSCAR sings the first lines of Vanilla Ice's 'Ice Ice Baby'.

CAITLIN: Seriously stop that; you're not funny.

OSCAR takes another bite of his sandwich.

[*Snatching his sandwich*] From now on, you can't eat. I can't eat; you can't eat.

OSCAR: Why can't I eat?

CAITLIN throws it as far as she can.

What if I get hungry?

CAITLIN: Tough.

OSCAR: Are you anorexic?

CAITLIN: What planet are you on?

OSCAR: Hunger World. Where normal people visit three times a day.

CAITLIN: You can't just ask girls if they're anorexic.

OSCAR: No judgement.

CAITLIN: I'm not anorexic.

OSCAR: Is that why you haven't been at school the past three weeks? Coz you're anorexic.

CAITLIN: I'm having an operation tomorrow, alright? And I'm not allowed to eat or drink anything before surgery.

OSCAR: What kind of operation?

CAITLIN: A boob job.

OSCAR: Oh.

CAITLIN: Oh my God, I'm not getting a boob job, that was a joke!

OSCAR: Hey, Caitlin?

CAITLIN: What?

OSCAR: Did you cut yourself?

CAITLIN: …

OSCAR: The gash on your leg.

CAITLIN: What do you think?

OSCAR: Doesn't it hurt?

CAITLIN: Nah, it feels nice.

OSCAR: I don't get it.

CAITLIN: It's from Mike's party.

OSCAR: Oh. Yeah, I heard you fell over.

CAITLIN: Yeah.

OSCAR: I heard you got so drunk you were crawling round on all fours.

CAITLIN: Well, that's not what happened.

OSCAR: So what happened?

CAITLIN: Shut up, dick cheese.

OSCAR: Looks pretty nasty.

CAITLIN: My knee just buckled when I was dancing. I wasn't drunk. I mean I *was* drunk, but that's not why I was on the floor.

OSCAR: Wouldn't know; wasn't invited.

CAITLIN: Have you talked to literally anyone this term? If you wanna get invited to things you have to actually talk to people.

OSCAR: I'm talking to you.

CAITLIN: Well, it was totally shit, okay, no-one freaking helped me, even though I was clearly in pain, they were just laughing and thought it was funny but it actually effing killed. So thanks for bringing it up.

OSCAR: …

You know what'll cheer you up?

CAITLIN: LOL cats?

OSCAR: Mum gave me fifteen bucks for lunch today. Which I didn't spend. Coz I made a sandwich. I'm thrifty like that. So you wanna go get Macca's for dinner? My shout. So long as it's under fifteen dollars.

CAITLIN: I have Mum's credit card, so it's cool.

OSCAR: Well, you wanna get Macca's together anyway?

CAITLIN: Nah, let's do something crazy.

OSCAR: KFC?

CAITLIN: No, something totally mental. Something big. Something way beyond what anyone ever reckoned we could.

OSCAR: And waste a perfectly good TV-watching afternoon?

CAITLIN: That is the saddest thing I've ever heard.

OSCAR: Don't fix it if it ain't broke.

CAITLIN: Well, everything *is* broken, alright? Mum's being totally mental. My friends suck. You're boring. And life is totally completely unfair.

OSCAR: Well, if everything's so awful and you're so angry about it why don't you just leave.

CAITLIN: Maybe I will.

OSCAR: Good luck with that.

CAITLIN: Good luck with learning to wipe your own asshole.

OSCAR: Not one of your bests.

>   *Pause.*

CAITLIN: Maybe I *should* just run away. Mess everything up and see if anything changes. If I make enough of a mess.

OSCAR: Don't be thick.

CAITLIN: We could though. Think about it. No-one knows we're here. We could just totally run away. Go full-on missing.

OSCAR: I don't wanna go missing.

CAITLIN: Because your life is *so* great?

OSCAR: What's wrong with my life?

CAITLIN: It's a nightmare. It's worse than mine.

OSCAR: It's not that bad.

CAITLIN: Oscar, you sit by yourself every single day looking totally miserable and sorry for yourself. You slink around corridors. You eat lunch in the teachers' staffroom! You're so weird. You don't even try to be normal.

OSCAR: Because no-one likes me, okay, it's shit! Why would I *push* myself on people that don't even like me?

CAITLIN: You don't even *try.* I can't make people be friends with you if you don't even try to act normal.

OSCAR: Well, I'm not normal anymore, Caitlin. Nothing about my life feels normal. Hunter topped himself, and now I'm like suicide boy, and I don't think anything will ever be normal for me again.

CAITLIN: So let's run away. Just us. We could actually have the most hectic adventure of our lives.

OSCAR: Just outta nowhere?

CAITLIN: Look. I'm sorry. We're clearly incapable of being friends at the moment. But something happened today, and now if I go home I'm in really, really deep trouble.

OSCAR: What did you do?

CAITLIN: I don't wanna talk about it. Please, Oscar? Don't you miss hanging out?

OSCAR: Okay. But I need to get permission first—

CAITLIN: No! You have to swear, Oscar, that no matter what, you won't tell anyone where we go.

OSCAR: Why not?

CAITLIN: I mean it.

OSCAR: …

CAITLIN: Swear.

OSCAR: I swear.

CAITLIN: Let's make a blood pact.

OSCAR: You don't believe me?

CAITLIN: Swear on our blood that you won't tell anyone where we go.

OSCAR: We're gonna hav'ta go home eventually.

CAITLIN: Do it.

OSCAR: Well then, then, you hav'ta swear that we really will be friends again.

CAITLIN: What?

OSCAR: And you're not gonna back out.

CAITLIN: I won't.

OSCAR: For real. You have to swear you aren't gonna ditch me. And I don't mean now, I mean, like, when things go back to normal you won't disappear again.

CAITLIN: I promise.

OSCAR: Swear.

> CAITLIN *takes a broken Coke bottle from the ground. Cuts her palm.*

CAITLIN: Cross my heart.

> OSCAR *takes it from her.*

OSCAR: [*cutting his palm*] Ouch.

> *They hold their hands palm to palm.*

Caitlin Dickens, I swear on the life of Kanye West, that I will never, no matter what, ever, dob us in.

CAITLIN: Oscar Jackson, I swear to you, on my most treasured collection of Taylor Swift paraphernalia, that when we go back to normal, we'll be friends again.

OSCAR: Okay, let's do it. Let's go missing.

CAITLIN: You mean it?

OSCAR: Can you drive a manual?

CAITLIN: I got my L's.

OSCAR: Alright. See that truck over there?

CAITLIN: Yeah.

OSCAR: Your chariot awaits.

CAITLIN: Are you serious?

OSCAR: Dead serious.

CAITLIN: Oscar Jackson, you kleptomaniac.

OSCAR: We're running.

CAITLIN: Yep.

OSCAR: Deal.

END OF SCENE ONE

SCENE TWO

Midnight.

A dingy room at a highway motor inn. A double bed with a mustard-coloured dust cover. An old television mounted to the wall (perhaps hanging crooked from a previous occupant's attempt to pry it off). Ugly art hangs above the bedhead.

CAITLIN enters with her backpack. She checks her reflection in the mirror. Decides to reapply lip gloss. She looks into her eyes in the reflection, then inhales and exhales with determination.

OSCAR enters. Dumps his backpack on the floor. Surveys the room. Checks out the bathroom.

OSCAR: [*offstage*] *Yuckkkk!*

> *He re-enters.*

Don't go in there, it stinks! Someone didn't flush.

CAITLIN: Bog bandit. Go flush it down.

OSCAR: You go flush it down.

CAITLIN: I don't want to flush someone else's shit.

OSCAR: Neither do I.

CAITLIN: Go flush or it'll stink up this room too.

OSCAR: Too late for that.

CAITLIN: You're the one who found it.

OSCAR: No, Cate, it's so rank, it looks like it's been there for days, it's all coming apart and dissolving into these tinier pieces that are turning the water brown.

CAITLIN: Alright / stop talking about it—

OSCAR: Pleeeeeeeeeeease?

CAITLIN: Alright! I'll do it.

> *Wrapping her arm over her face, she goes into the bathroom and flushes. Then re-enters.*

You massive wimp, you owe me for that. Way to make a girl feel special.

*She goes to wash her hands in the kitchen basin, turns on the tap.
Water spurts out inconsistently and brown. She squeals.*

OSCAR: This is rank. We can't sleep here.

CAITLIN: We have to.

OSCAR: Let's go back to my house.

CAITLIN: C'mon, it's not that bad.

OSCAR: Not that bad?! The carpet smells like a urinal cake.

CAITLIN: Imagine you're somewhere else.

OSCAR: I can't.

CAITLIN: Just close your eyes, and pretend we're someplace awesome.

OSCAR: [*eyes shut tightly*] … It's not working. My imagination's been destroyed by my iPad. I knew this'd get me one day.

CAITLIN: It's just for one night.

OSCAR: Let's sleep in the car.

CAITLIN: We can't, it's stolen. We'd be practically framing ourselves if anyone spots it.

OSCAR: It's worth it not to sleep on that mattress.

CAITLIN: You're right, probably has bed bugs. They'll crawl all over you while you're asleep at night, feasting on your hairy legs—

OSCAR: Eww, don't touch me with your poo hands.

CAITLIN: [*lurching at him*] You mean *these*!

OSCAR: Your precious, milky skin deserves the cosiest flannelette sheets.

CAITLIN: Mmmmm—

OSCAR: And melon-scented fabric softener.

CAITLIN: We're staying.

OSCAR: Alright. But you better have something planned that doesn't require using our imaginations.

CAITLIN: Chill. I'm totally down with the fact that imagination is consistently the biggest let-down. Hey, they have Foxtel here. Pretty fancy.

OSCAR: Ex-ex-ex adult vids, twenty-five bucks.

CAITLIN: You got twenty-five bucks?

OSCAR: Eww, not for nineties motel porn.

CAITLIN: We could make our own.

OSCAR: Oh my God, you sex addict, stop trying to do it with me.

CAITLIN: No idea what you're talking about.

OSCAR: You're totally creeping me out. I can't tell if you're being serious or not.

CAITLIN: You're blushing.

OSCAR: I'm not, I get sweaty, we've been through this.

>   *Pause.*

You know Mike Sanders said he couldn't fit his … you know … inside a toilet paper roll … because it's too big to fit inside.

CAITLIN: So what?

OSCAR: Do you think that's true?

CAITLIN: I don't know.

OSCAR: But if you had to guess?

CAITLIN: I really have no idea.

OSCAR: Do you think that's cool?

CAITLIN: I think you think it's cool.

OSCAR: I mean I've never tried, but I think mine would fit. My penis I mean.

CAITLIN: Oh-my-God-why-are-you-saying-this?

OSCAR: Are you uncomfortable.

CAITLIN: No.

OSCAR: You've gone all red.

CAITLIN: Shut up, dickhead.

OSCAR: You really have no opinion about Mike?

CAITLIN: Correct.

OSCAR: Well, that's funny, because I heard that you and Mike, well, you and a couple of guys, at the Year Ten formal, you snuck into the disabled toilet and gave anyone who wanted a blow job, and you gave like, thirty blow jobs that night.

CAITLIN: It's not true.

>   OSCAR *gives her an 'I don't believe you' look.*

It's not true. And whatever else Knob-Cheese-Mike said about me probably isn't true either, so you should probably just forget it.

OSCAR: …

CAITLIN: You wanna know what I've heard about you?

OSCAR: …

CAITLIN: I heard that you took a packet of Panadol in the school toilets and they caught you throwing it up.

OSCAR: How would you know? You haven't even been at school.

>   *Silence.*

Caitlin?

CAITLIN: Yes?

OSCAR: Never mind.

Long pause.

Actually, Caitlin?

CAITLIN: [*a mocking voice*] Caitlin.

OSCAR: Do you even like me?

CAITLIN: Stop fishing.

OSCAR: Because you swore you wouldn't ditch me.

CAITLIN: Well, I'm spontaneous, okay. I'm totally unpredictable.

OSCAR: You're not that unpredictable. Bit of a cliché actually.

CAITLIN: It's called being normal, Oscar. It's like one second everything is really funny, then the next you're really depressed, and then you're really angry. You can't be just one thing. It's always like fifty thousand, which is why it's completely impossible being seventeen.

OSCAR spots something behind the bed. He immediately jumps away.

OSCAR: What the—? *Yuck!* Is that—?

He pokes it with his foot.

Okay, do *not* come over here.

CAITLIN: What?

OSCAR: You don't wanna know.

CAITLIN: *What?!*

OSCAR: I'm pretty sure a rat tried to chew through the TV cable. I think it's a rat? An unidentified mammal. It's melted into the carpet.

CAITLIN: Gross. Show me.

OSCAR: Could be a baby possum, I guess. A little ringtail? That's sadder. Poor guy.

Pause.

This is the worst adventure ever.

CAITLIN: Well, it's not like we can drive back now, it's midnight.

OSCAR: Missed mocks for nothin'.

CAITLIN: Chill out, we got the whole night ahead of us.

OSCAR: I guess.

Pause.

So are we gonna sleep in the same bed?

CAITLIN: What do you wanna do?

OSCAR: It wouldn't be weird?

CAITLIN: I don't care.

OSCAR: I guess we can top and tail.

CAITLIN: Why'd your voice go funny?

OSCAR: *I* feel guilty.

CAITLIN: Bit late for that.

OSCAR: Don't *you* feel weird about it?

CAITLIN: You weren't having second thoughts when you were shoving your tongue down my throat at the park.

OSCAR: I panicked!

CAITLIN: That's not how normal people react to panic. Sucking on someone's face. Meanwhile, you were there within minutes after I texted, so don't pretend to be all innocent.

OSCAR: I was happy you were talkin' t' me again. Because you've actually been a total nightmare since—

CAITLIN: I don't wanna talk about Hunter. He freaking killed himself. That's seriously depressing, and we're here to have fun, so let's have fun.

> CAITLIN *takes a can of spray paint from her backpack. Neon pink. Starts tagging the walls. Wildflowers sprouting up from the skirting boards.*

OSCAR: You're literally mental.

CAITLIN: Eugh, everyone's always calling me mental, it's getting kinda boring.

OSCAR: So stop telling people to meet you in parks and they'll stop calling you mental.

CAITLIN: What's so bad about parks?

OSCAR: 'Oscar. Full stop. Wanna fuck. Question mark. Maluka Park.'

CAITLIN: There's already shit clogging up the toilet and freaking possum abortions on the floor. I'm making this place wayyyyyy less depressing. Here.

> *She extends the can to* OSCAR.

Trace me.

OSCAR: I'll pass.

CAITLIN: I dare you.

OSCAR: It's vandalism.

CAITLIN: You're not going to jail.

OSCAR: For a principal's kid, you have zero concept of the legal system.

CAITLIN: Yawn. Must be thrilling being you, Os.

> OSCAR *takes the spray paint from her.*

> CAITLIN *stands flat to the wall with her arms outstretched.*

Don't get it on my Converse, or you're dead to me.

> OSCAR *traces her silhouette carefully, nervous to be so close to her body.* CAITLIN *stands away from the wall, admires his work.*

It's me.

OSCAR: Yeah, if you were a two-dimensional ugly mistake—Oh wait! You already are.

CAITLIN: Alright, I'll let you have that one.

> *She touches the silhouette. Traces her fingers along the outline. She aligns her body back up with the drawing. Presses herself into the wall. Closes her eyes.*

[*Eyes still closed*] Sometimes I wish the world would just swallow me up.

OSCAR: Me too.

CAITLIN: Join the club.

OSCAR: The earth could swallow us up, you know, it's not impossible. It's highly, highly, highly improbable, but it could. Like when I touch your hand now …

> *He stands next to* CAITLIN *on the wall, mirroring her position, and presses his palm (the same palms as their blood pact) against hers.*

… my atoms are mixing with your atoms. Forced molecular penetration.

CAITLIN: [*leaving her hand there*] Yikes, Oscar, stop raping me.

OSCAR: There's no edge of you, or me, or the walls, or the ceiling. Fuzzy edges. So we're all interconnected.

CAITLIN: Musta wagged science that day.

OSCAR: Didn't learn that in science. Hunter told me.

> *He takes the spray paint, paints a crown on the silhouette.*

Royalty.

CAITLIN: A queen.

OSCAR: [*bowing to her*] Your highness.

CAITLIN: Queen Nightshade.

OSCAR: A queen without a kingdom.

CAITLIN: She does. Not here but. This would be the most depressing palace ever. On a cliff. Overlooking a beach. At the edge of a desert. Between the tiny cosmic barrier where the desert meets the ocean. Red-hot sand beneath her feet. And the sun burns so bright you'd think the whole world was on fire.

> *Club beats blast. The Presets' 'Girl and the Sea'.* CAITLIN *is transported to another world.*
>
> *The silhouette bursts with wildflowers.*
>
> CAITLIN *spies her deadly nightshade tattoo on the silhouette. She compares the two. The silhouette pulses at her touch.*

Ouch! What the—
Ooooooouch!

> *A glowing thorn from the deadly nightshade has punctured the wound on her leg. She pulls it out.*

[*Exhaling sharply*] Ah.

> *Blood trickles down her leg.*
>
> CAITLIN *dances, with her eyes closed, to The Presets' 'Girl and the Sea' which plays impossibly loud now.*

The music pulsing through my bones. So loud it fills up my brain and crowds out my thoughts. My head's pounding from the amphetamine. Dancing so fast you'd think the whole world was on fire.

And then, this is when it happens. This fucking explosion in my knee.

My skin rips apart and I see can my bones, and they've turned to ash, crumbling, and I fall fast and hard to the floor. My hands stretch out to catch me and smash right through the floorboards. Fuzzy edges. Through the concrete, and the whole room rips apart.

And I'm in the desert and I'm free. I'm fucking free. Red-hot sand beneath my feet and I'm running. Running fast as I can. Away from parents. Away from hospitals. Away from bullshit doctors. And clipboards. And medical results.

Searching for somewhere, a place to dance. A place to get the fuck away.

I arrive at a clearing, through the twisting roots of mangroves. Out of nowhere, giant banksias with stems twice as thick as my body *sprout* out of the earth's mouth. Red and bright and angry. Flowers like this mean business. Flowers like this don't fuck around.

I can smell the salt.
The air's gone salty.
I'm getting close.
Closer to the sea.
Closer to the cosmic barrier where the desert tumbles into the ocean.

OSCAR: Caitlin?
CAITLIN: What?
OSCAR: Caitlin?
CAITLIN: Not now, Oscar!
OSCAR: Caitlin, d'you want Milo or Nesquick?
CAITLIN: I said not *now*!

> *The world vanishes and* CAITLIN *is back in the motel.*

> OSCAR *sits cross-legged on the bed, sipping hot chocolate.*

OSCAR: Mmmm, hot chocolate.
CAITLIN: Nesquick or Milo?
OSCAR: Two scoops of each.
CAITLIN: Yum.
OSCAR: Made extra.

> CAITLIN *joins him. They top and tail. Sipping their hot drinks.*

CAITLIN: I doubted you at first, but this is exactly what I needed.
OSCAR: There aren't any pink marshmallows left now. But the white ones are perfect. They look like little goopy clouds.
CAITLIN: Swirling around in a chocolate sky. Lucky things.
OSCAR: No idea of their fate.
CAITLIN: Bliss. I think I'd like to stay here forever.
OSCAR: They'll kick us out eventually.
CAITLIN: Who?
OSCAR: You know.

CAITLIN: The maids?

OSCAR: Yeah, but I don't think you're s'posed to call them 'maids'.

CAITLIN: It's not like they're a race of people.

OSCAR: Still, they'll come, label or no label.

CAITLIN: Maybe they won't. What if they never show up? What if the whole world turned to ash, and it were just you and me, and this room, and this single, last marshmallow?

OSCAR: Would you let me eat it?

CAITLIN: Desperate times, Oscar.

OSCAR: Or would you split it fifty-fifty?

CAITLIN: Hmmmmmmmm.

OSCAR: Or eat it all yourself?

CAITLIN: [*as in 'correct'*] Ding ding ding!

OSCAR: There are worse sins.

CAITLIN: Like terrorism. Or preferring Marmite. Or murder.

OSCAR: D'you reckon you could murder someone?

CAITLIN: No way.

OSCAR: Think about it, though. If they were gonna kill me.

CAITLIN: Nup.

OSCAR: Really think about it.

CAITLIN: Ummmmm. No. Sorry not sorry.

OSCAR: Not even to save my life?

CAITLIN: Okay maybe.

OSCAR: I'd do it for you.

CAITLIN: I said maybe.

OSCAR: I could do it for sure.

CAITLIN: As if.

OSCAR: I would. Under the right circumstances. If I were angry enough. If someone took something away from me, and it made me so furious that I completely lost it. I think everyone could. If you found the right trigger.

CAITLIN: Well, that's comforting.

   Pause.

When I was eight I killed my cousin's turtle.

OSCAR: On purpose?

CAITLIN: Sort of.

OSCAR: I'm impressed.

CAITLIN: I was convinced I was actually a mermaid, so I took it into the bath to see if it'd start talking to me. And my cousin, Jess, she had this banana-scented bubble bath, smelled like banana paddle-pop. It was the best. So I put loads in, and was splashin' round and all that. And then outta nowhere, the turtle started going mental. Darting around and snapping at me. I started screaming and kicking at it, and jumped outta the bath. And I looked back, and the turtle was just floating there.

OSCAR: …

CAITLIN: I guess I poisoned it with the bubble bath.

OSCAR: Well, that's depressing.

CAITLIN: It's funny!

OSCAR: Did you bury it somewhere?

CAITLIN: I tried hiding it in Granny's room and found a drawer filled with arthritis medication and dildos. Got in heaps of trouble. Mum cracked the shits, and my psycho freak bitch auntie said *Woman's Day* did this whole cover issue on signs that your child's a psychopath. And killing the family pet was like the number one sign. So Mum was, like, *unusually* nice to me that week.

OSCAR: Parents are way more scared of us than we are of them.

CAITLIN: For sure.

OSCAR: If I ever did somethin' messed, like on another level messed, Mum'd take the fall for me coz she loves me too hard. But if she ever did something, something truly awful, she'd never let me take the blame. It's like win-win.

CAITLIN: Your face is like win-win.

OSCAR: I'll take that as a compliment.

CAITLIN: It was meant to be a compliment.

OSCAR: Oh.

> *He smiles.*

Can I show you something?

CAITLIN: Depends.

OSCAR: It's pretty much the most valuable thing I own.

CAITLIN: If it's a body part then I definitely don't need to see it.

OSCAR: Yeah, yeah.

OSCAR *carefully takes a graphic novel from inside his backpack.*

CAITLIN: What is it?

OSCAR: Only the best graphic novel in existence.

CAITLIN: A what?

OSCAR: A graphic novel.

CAITLIN: Like a kid's book?

OSCAR: No, a graphic novel is like a novel with hectic graphics in a comic book layout.

CAITLIN: Sounds like a kid's book.

OSCAR: It's a really rare edition. You're pretty lucky to get to hold it actually. Cool, huh? I knew you'd dig it.

CAITLIN: [*reading the cover*] *Hell's Canyon*. Didn't know you collected baby stuff.

OSCAR: I don't.

CAITLIN: Hey, I recognise these pictures.

OSCAR: *Hell's Canyon*? There's a whole fantasy series.

CAITLIN: No, I know that place. That place in the drawings. It's a real place.

OSCAR: You've read it before? I musta read it a thousand times.

CAITLIN: I mean I've been there. I was literally *just there*. The sand and the rocks and the twisting mangroves—

OSCAR: Hey, be careful with the pages—

CAITLIN: It's a real place. In Broome. Ages away from here. Totally isolated, right on the edge of a cliff.

OSCAR: As if.

CAITLIN: We could go stand there. Right in the depths of it. Right inside the comic. We're going. We have to go.

OSCAR: Stand in the pages.

CAITLIN: Where did you get this?

OSCAR: ... It was Hunter's

CAITLIN *closes the book and stares at it. She's upset.*

CAITLIN: You just carry it around with you? That's really pathetic. Why'd you even show it to me?!

She throws the book hard at the wall.

OSCAR: *Hey!* What's your problem?!

CAITLIN: It's a stupid comic!

OSCAR: [*picking it up*] Use your brain.

CAITLIN: I have a brain.

OSCAR: The cover's gone all crinkled.

CAITLIN: I have a brain!

OSCAR: I told you it was rare.

CAITLIN: I told you I didn't want to talk about Hunter.

OSCAR: Why not?

CAITLIN: Because it's depressing.

OSCAR: It's still a part of me.

CAITLIN: No it's not. It doesn't have to be. It doesn't have to define you.

OSCAR: I can't help it. Sometimes there are things you can't forget about even when you try. They show up in your brain outta nowhere. Walking home, or in the line at the canteen, or when we were making out before. It smacks you right in the face. Right outta nowhere ... I don't know what's so wrong about remembering.

CAITLIN: Well, try harder to forget.

OSCAR: I don't want to.

> Silence. OSCAR is *clearly upset.*

I don't want to forget.

It's like a part of me likes that right now everything is so weird and shit and horrible. Because that's what it is.

I don't want it to become normal, that he's gone.

> CAITLIN *sits next to him, tries to take the book from him. He holds onto it.*

What?

CAITLIN: I wanna see.

OSCAR: You already saw it.

CAITLIN: I wanna remember.

> OSCAR *passes it to her.* CAITLIN *flips through the pages.*

I heard you found him.

OSCAR: That's what the rumors round school were.

CAITLIN: Yeah. That you found him swinging in the garage.

OSCAR: ...

That's not what happened.

...

You started the rumours, didn't you?

Long pause.

CAITLIN: It was nice that it wasn't me bein' talked about that week.

OSCAR: That's pretty shit of you.

CAITLIN: How'd you know it was me?

OSCAR: No-one else'd been in his room. The details. Made sense it was you.

CAITLIN: Oh.

OSCAR: ...

CAITLIN: So you didn't find him?

OSCAR: ...

CAITLIN: You didn't see anything?

OSCAR: Stop.

CAITLIN: What?

OSCAR: Pressuring me. Bullying me—

CAITLIN: I'm not.

OSCAR: Yes you are.

CAITLIN: I'm not a bully.

OSCAR: Is that a joke?

CAITLIN: I'm just messing when I talk like that. That's how I talk with my friends.

OSCAR: Well, sometimes it doesn't feel like you're just messing, sometimes it feels like you genuinely believe you're better than me.

CAITLIN: Well, I don't.

OSCAR: That's not an apology.

CAITLIN: I'm *sorry*.

OSCAR: Forget it.

CAITLIN: I am. I get it.

OSCAR: No you don't.

CAITLIN: Yeah I do, Hunter was a really shitty boyfriend. So I get it. And I'm sorry.

OSCAR: You threw me under the bus.

CAITLIN: I know.

OSCAR: You literally *made stuff up* about me finding him, so you didn't have to deal with it.

CAITLIN: Because I fuckin' hated Hunter, alright! He was always cheating on me, and talking shit. I didn't want to be known as the dead guy's girlfriend.

OSCAR: Well, he's still my brother, so you don't have to talk like he deserved it or something.

CAITLIN: You know I saw him that day. The day he did it.

OSCAR: …

CAITLIN: Down the shops. He asked me for a smoke.

OSCAR: Did he seem … I mean was he acting like—

CAITLIN: Nah. He didn't seem like anything.

OSCAR: …

CAITLIN: Oscar, you're a million times better than him, and I like you way more.

OSCAR: It's not a competition.

CAITLIN: I'm not making it a competition

OSCAR: Well, you don't have to compare it.

CAITLIN: Alright! I'm sorry. I mean it. About saying those things. I'd take it back if I could. No more lies. I swear.

OSCAR: It pretty much ruined our friendship.

CAITLIN: Yeah.

> *Pause.*

But we've got it back now, hey?

OSCAR: Yeah.

> *Pause.*

[*American accent*] Caitlin and Oscar: The Awesome Squad.

CAITLIN: That's absolutely not our name.

OSCAR: [*American accent*] The Awesome Squad, back together at last.

CAITLIN: Please never say that in public.

OSCAR: Say what?

CAITLIN: If you / say it—

OSCAR: Oh, you mean The Awesome Squad. We should go on an actual adventure, hey? To Hell's Canyon.

CAITLIN: Yeah.

OSCAR: Or anywhere. And not tomorrow, I mean just anytime. Just coz. And actually do it properly. With plans and snacks and stuff.

CAITLIN: Yeah, an actual adventure way less lame than this one.

OSCAR: You mean you're not enjoying the possum abortion and poo water and piss stains on the carpet?

CAITLIN: Stop it, talkin' like that, you're turning me on.

OSCAR: We can go to Hell's Canyon and stand in the pages like you said. And do actual fun stuff, like swimming and hiking and snorkelling—

CAITLIN: Hey, Oscar?

OSCAR: Yeah?

CAITLIN: I can't do those things with you.

OSCAR: Yes you can.

CAITLIN: I can't go swimming and stuff.

OSCAR: Okay. Why not?

CAITLIN: Because I just can't, okay.

OSCAR: You don't want to, you mean?

CAITLIN: No, I mean … I don't know if I can anymore.

OSCAR: You backing out?

CAITLIN: Did I say I was backing out?

OSCAR: Because you swore you wouldn't ditch me.

CAITLIN: Are you even listening?

> *The neon world reveals itself to* CAITLIN. *The desert leaks through the walls.*

OSCAR: You're backing out even though you promised this was for real.

CAITLIN: This is for real.

OSCAR: Because I actually like hanging out with you.

CAITLIN: I do too. I really, really like you, Oscar.

OSCAR: So what's the big deal with daydreaming and planning and having things to look forward to?

CAITLIN: It's embarrassing—

OSCAR: What? Is it so completely humiliating to like me?

> *Wildflowers glow hot and bright.*

CAITLIN: That's not what I said. You're not even listening to me.

OSCAR: You're not better than me, Caitlin. You're not better than anyone. You're just as rubbish as everyone else we know.

CAITLIN: Shut up, I need to think—I need to tell you 'bout something—

> CAITLIN *is sucked back into the desert.*

Wait!

The walls covered in nightshade won't let her through. The silhou-
ette starts to bleed from the leg.

[*Touching the silhouette*] You're leaking.

She looks at the blood on her fingers.

It's disgusting!

Blinding pink light swallows her.

On the couch under my doona. Presets blasting on my iPod.
Mum's out getting hot pies, and Red Bull, and chocolate, and
magazines—anything to distract me.
My phone screen flashes up— [*the hospital*]
Unknown number.
Not now. Where's Mum?
Block call.
Flashing again. Unknown number.
Block.
Flashing again. One voicemail received.
Delete.
This is bullshit. It's not fair.
I didn't do anything.
I could torch the house. Torch the whole freaking school with eve-
ryone in it. See how they react. With grace and dignity? Yeah right.

Mum, get the fuck back from the shops; I don't want a dirty pie.

Turn my iPod way up. Slam my head into my pillow and the fuzzy
edges dissolve the couch into a thousand tiny pieces of light and I'm
racing back through time.

Back to the day Hunter did it.

I'm at the shops near my house, and a guy comes over, taller than me,
stinks like bourbon and pot; know that stench from a mile away. He's
eyes are rolling back in his head, and he asks me for a durry.

'Get your own smokes, Hunter, you scab.'
[*As Hunter*] 'Fuck you, you fat fucking cunt, gimme one.'
[*As CAITLIN*] 'You povo bogan shit! You wouldn't even exist if your
mum had enough money for an abortion.'

This that one gets to him. Awesome.

Then his face changes, and he spits in my hair.

And I feel fire well up in my belly and pour out of my mouth.

I pick up my backpack and smash him as hard as I can in the face.

He's caught off guard and stumbles back. And I keep smashing him and smashing him. He'll bash me the second I stop, Caitlin don't stop just keep going.

Until his massive body softens, and his shoulders relax, and he's crying. Like really, really cryin'. Tears and snot and stuff. His face is all screwed up like a fucking pug dog.

This is my chance.

And I take it.

And I run.

In the clearing again. Through the dirt, through mud, the insects, the rocks. Can smell the moisture on the mangrove leaves.

The temperature drops and my arms and legs are covered in goose-bumps.

I'm so close.

I'm so fucking close to the ocean.

> *The silhouette of* CAITLIN *bleeds from the leg. Blood trickles down the wall.*

You're leaking. Poor thing.

It's disgusting.

It's repulsive.

Stuck in the desert with nothin' but your stupid ideas and your ugly face and your bleeding heart.

> *The motel room forces itself back. The room is torn apart. Evidence of an ugly fight.*

[*Screaming in pain*] Ahhhh! My skin's burning. My skin's burning it really hurts.

OSCAR: Okay okay / okay okay—

CAITLIN: My leg—Make it stop, Oscar.

OSCAR: What the—

CAITLIN: My leg's on fire, Oscar, it's on fire, it's burning, it's going to turn to ash—

OSCAR: Cate, you're burning up.

CAITLIN: Don't touch it, you'll / make it worse, you'll make it worse if you touch me, Oscar *don't*!

OSCAR: Caitlin, I don't know, I don't know what I'm supposed to do! Let's get you under the shower. I'm gonna lift you, okay?

CAITLIN: *Stop!*

OSCAR: On three—

CAITLIN: *Oscar, I don't / want you to!*

OSCAR: One. Two. Three.

CAITLIN: *Don't touch me!*

> OSCAR *lifts her into his arms.* CAITLIN *struggles and they both fall hard to the ground.* CAITLIN *screams in pain.*

OSCAR: I am so so so so so sorry.

> CAITLIN *'s gash on her knee pours with blood.*

Holy shit.

CAITLIN: My leg's gone fuzzy.

> OSCAR *peels back the plastic around her tattoo. A messy ragdoll wound.*

> CAITLIN *cries.*

OSCAR: [*rubbing her back*] Shhhh, shhhh, it's okay.

Shhhh—

It's just a gash.

It's just a small gash, you're okay.

Shhhh—

You're fine.

It's not the end of the world.

CAITLIN: It *is* the end of the world!

OSCAR: You're alright.

CAITLIN: It's all over my clothes.

OSCAR: You can shower.

CAITLIN: I want it off me.

OSCAR: We have our PE stuff. You're fine.

CAITLIN: Fuck off, I don't want your help!

> CAITLIN *hides in the bathroom. Slams the door.*

> OSCAR *stands outside, not knowing how to help.*

OSCAR: Caitlin?

CAITLIN: [*offstage*] Leave me alone!

OSCAR: What's going on?

CAITLIN: [*offstage*] Fuck off, I don't wanna fuckin' talk about it! Just take the car and leave, alright!

OSCAR: Hey, Cate?

CAITLIN: [*offstage*] I don't want you to be here anymore! It's ruined.

OSCAR: Nothing's ruined. We can literally pretend this never happened. I swear. I'll literally erase it from my memory right now. Deleted! Done.

CAITLIN: [*offstage*] I don't have any other clothes.

OSCAR: I do.

CAITLIN: [*offstage*] Can I have them?

OSCAR: Yep.

He goes to his bag. Takes out dirty, sweaty PE trackies. Probably hasn't washed them all term. Passes them through the bathroom door.

Hey, a girl's never worn my clothes before … so that's kinda cool.

CAITLIN: [*offstage*] And the deodorant in my backpack.

OSCAR *empties the contents of her backpack onto the bed. A pencil case covered in whiteout drawings, black nail polish, Impulse deodorant, and an A4 envelope.* OSCAR *grabs the deodorant, passes it through the door.*

He waits.

He spots something on the front of the envelope. He picks it up, studies the front, then slides the papers out. He reads them.

A moment passes.

CAITLIN *re-enters from the bathroom wearing* OSCAR*'s PE trackies. She sees* OSCAR *reading the papers. She freezes.*

OSCAR: Um, what date is it today?

CAITLIN: …

OSCAR: Is today the twenty-seventh?

CAITLIN: …

OSCAR: You have an appointment on the twenty-eighth.

CAITLIN: …

OSCAR: Um, scheduled for, um, eight a.m. Eight a.m. tomorrow morning.

CAITLIN: You went through my stuff?

OSCAR: Were you gonna tell me?

CAITLIN: That's private!

OSCAR: Were you going to tell me?

CAITLIN: I didn't give you permission to go through my personal belongings.

OSCAR: [*holding the letter to her*] When did you get this?

CAITLIN: It's not any of your business!

OSCAR: Don't lie.

CAITLIN: This morning. Ten a.m. this morning.

OSCAR: So what, *five hours* before you texted me? You don't talk to me for months and then that's why you're speaking to me out of nowhere.

CAITLIN: I'm sorry.

OSCAR: So what, what does this mean?

[*Reading*] Osteosarcoma? You're like … sick?

CAITLIN: …

OSCAR: Are you sick or something?

CAITLIN: They want to cut off my leg, Oscar. Depending on what happens they might just cut it off.

OSCAR: What?

CAITLIN: Bone cancer. In my knee. That's why I fell at the party. My knee's totally messed. They're gonna try to remove the tumor, but if it doesn't go well then it's like, see ya later, leg.

Pause.

OSCAR: You shoulda said something.

CAITLIN: I didn't know properly till this morning.

OSCAR: What the fuck is wrong with you?!

CAITLIN: Stop yelling at me.

OSCAR: You should have told me!

CAITLIN: I tried to—

OSCAR: You're a fucking liar.

CAITLIN: I didn't want anyone to know.

OSCAR: I genuinely thought you wanted to be to be my friend.

CAITLIN: I do. I do now.

OSCAR: Be honest, we never woulda come here, never woulda even *texted* me if you were healthy?

CAITLIN: …

OSCAR: Do you know how selfish that is? I would have come anyway, I would have done anything. You didn't have to lie. You didn't have to trick me into this—

CAITLIN: I'm sorry!

OSCAR: You have an appointment at eight a.m. We need to leave.

CAITLIN: I'm not going. I've decided. I'm not gonna do it. I'm running.

OSCAR: Caitlin, don't be dumb.

CAITLIN: I don't want to go back. I don't want to just close my eyes and hope for the best.

OSCAR: You're not gonna even try?!

CAITLIN: It's scary. If you just give me some time, then maybe / I can figure out what to do.

OSCAR: I can't believe you're doing this. You fucking did it again. You just keep making shit up and making shit up until it's one completely irreversible awful mess.

CAITLIN: Maybe there's something else we can do / and then I wouldn't have to—

OSCAR: Caitlin, can you stop talking for one *second* so we can figure out—

CAITLIN: What if I there was, though? Like you said, there's no edge of you or me / and when I hold your hand now, our atoms are mixing.

OSCAR: Caitlin, stop. Please just stop it. *Stop it!*

I need to think.

What happens if we don't get there at eight?

CAITLIN: [*miming slitting her throat*] Kkkkkkkk!

OSCAR: What?! Is that an effing joke?

CAITLIN: If I don't go.

OSCAR: Get your things.

CAITLIN: You know fuckin' / nothin' about—

OSCAR: Right now!

CAITLIN: Fine then. I'll go to Hell's Canyon alone.

OSCAR: No effing way! No *way*!

CAITLIN: You know best, do you?

OSCAR: You can't fix this by running away. Use your brain.

CAITLIN: You have alllllllll the answers?

OSCAR: I didn't say that.

CAITLIN: Because if you even try to tell me what I 'should' do I / swear I will seriously start fucking shit up.

OSCAR: I didn't say 'should' and I want to understand but we need to leave.

The operation's in three hours, the drive takes three and a half.

CAITLIN: I mean it. I'll fucking *kill myself* if you / don't give me a second to think.

OSCAR: Great choice of words there. Real fucking sensitive.

CAITLIN: I mean it.

OSCAR: Use your head.

CAITLIN: I don't *care*. I *know* that getting the operation is the logical thing to do, okay? I'm not stupid. I just don't *want* to because that's how I *feel*. And I'm sorry you don't *like* the way I feel, but I don't fucking care about doing the right thing, and I really don't give a shit about what anyone thinks about what I do.

I never have, so why would I start now?

OSCAR: Get in the car.

CAITLIN: I'm not gonna get in the car because I am fucking *angry*.

OSCAR: Stop yelling at me.

CAITLIN: Let's keep going, let's go right now to Hell's Canyon together. Let's pack up and go.

OSCAR: I think you should go to the hospital.

CAITLIN: Why?

OSCAR: Because I don't want to do this anymore.

CAITLIN: Nothing's changed.

OSCAR: What's changed is I didn't know you were having an operation *today* and I didn't know you had cancer and I didn't know that if you don't *get the operation* I am implicated in the consequences / and maybe if I knew that, I wouldn't be here in this insane mess you've made of it.

CAITLIN: Well, I'm sorry to *inconvenience* you! I'm sorry this is such a massive shock for you. That must feel really shit.

OSCAR: Alright. I'm leaving. Come or don't come.

CAITLIN: *Stop it!* Slow down. Everything keeps racing ahead of me whether I make a choice about it or not, and I can't seem to catch up. The world's completely raced ahead and it's fucking lonely back here being angry all by myself.

OSCAR: If you didn't want to feel lonely, then you should have told me the truth.

CAITLIN: I didn't want you to be my friend coz I was sick.

OSCAR: Funny, coz that pretty much sums up the *exact* reason you asked me.

CAITLIN: I asked you because I wanted you to love me before you had a reason to.

OSCAR: Well, I don't love you anymore.

> *Long pause.*

CAITLIN: We can still do this.

OSCAR: I don't want to.

CAITLIN: Can you please just—
Hold up a second—
Can you please—
Can you swear on our friendship that you'll give me some more time to figure out—

OSCAR: There's no *friendship* to swear on, Caitlin. Not anymore.

> OSCAR *leaves.*

> *An explosion of light.*

> *Silence.*

> *Deep under water.* CAITLIN *watches as the light on the surface of the water ripples across space. The ocean bursts from the drawer in the bedside table.*

> *A turtle lands at* CAITLIN *'s feet.*

CAITLIN: Merlin? Hey, little guy. Sorry I killed you. There are worse things I guess. Oh, I packed us something.

> *She takes two bright yellow floaties from her backpack.*

A flotation device. In case of emergency.

> *She puts them on.*

It's safer this way. More buoyant.

> *She lies down in a puddle next to the turtle. She attempts backstroke. It's pointless in such a small amount of water.*

Useless. Like all my plans.

She stabs the floaties with the deadly nightshade thorn. The floaties explode with shimmering glitter.

I feel sick.
Gross and heavy.
My useless, cloudy heart and foggy brain.
Couldn't sit up even if I wanted to.
Your fucking stupid voice,
'There's no friendship to swear on, Caitlin',
smashes me in the chest.
And I'm falling—
backwards—
off a cliff—
hurtling towards the sea—
right toward the cosmic barrier where the desert and the ocean meet.
A tiny delicate force field where two worlds are fuzzily forced together.
Fuzzy edges.
It's precious, and my heavy body smashes through it.
Breaks it apart.
And I'm sucked down beneath the waves.
Water's filling up my mouth and nose and ears and chest and lungs,
'I can't fucking breath now, Oscar you dog.'
Bones heavy with water, weighed down by grief—
forced down into a watery world of despair.

Right into the depths of the canyon.

Plonk.

Pause.

At least I'm alone here.

Pause.

CAITLIN *wriggles uncomfortably. She pulls two big handfuls of wet, red sand from inside her pockets, from inside her shoes, from in her hair.*

Sand. Hell's Canyon.

OSCAR *appears in* CAITLIN'*s kingdom.*

OSCAR: Hey, girl.

CAITLIN: Fuck off.

OSCAR: Caitlin, get up.

CAITLIN: Get outta my kingdom, okay, you're not allowed in here.

OSCAR: I'm sorry I said those things.

CAITLIN: Apology not accepted.

OSCAR: Are you irreversibly angry with me?

CAITLIN: How does it all end? For me I mean.

OSCAR: Don't know yet.

CAITLIN: What about for Hunter?

OSCAR: Gone.

CAITLIN: How'd he do it?

OSCAR: With an electrical cord. Swung it over the support beam in the garage.

CAITLIN: No electrical cords at the bottom of the ocean.

OSCAR: No support beams either. You'll have to make a choice.

CAITLIN: Just slip away I guess. Wait until the fish eat me, and I'm nothin' but teeth and bones and an ugly starfish belly-bar.

OSCAR: Or we could swim to the surface?

CAITLIN: I'm too heavy.

OSCAR: I can swim for two.

CAITLIN: It's scary.

OSCAR: Gotta decide soon, but. Need to hitch a ride while the tide's still in.

CAITLIN: I don't want to. I don't want to just hope for the best. I hate not knowing what's gonna happen before it happens.

OSCAR: You'll figure it out.

CAITLIN: Nah, not this.

And my body shrinks and I'm wearing a Finding Nemo rashie.
I'm swimming with Mum; she's teaching me to bodysurf.
I'm on the top of the swell, but I can't kick fast enough.
I'm kicking and kicking, but it's no use.
I'm too little to outsmart this massive wave.
I topple headfirst over the top, and it dunks me, sucking me under, my body's spinning outta control and I genuinely think I'm gonna drown.
I suddenly realise that if I don't breathe, that if I don't get air, then …

But then my cheek hits the sand, and the wave washes away, and I'm fine, but I'm crying.

My tears wash me all the way back to my bedroom, and I'm on the couch with Mum. She's sitting next to me and she says,
'When you think your heart might break.
Let it.
It's hard for the world to get bigger
when you're clinging to a piece that's about to break.
So let it break,
and let it break open.'

OSCAR: Caitlin?

CAITLIN: There's no way out.

OSCAR: There is.

CAITLIN: Even from this?

OSCAR: Yeah. Even this.

CAITLIN: What if it doesn't work?

> OSCAR *swims to the surface.*

Hello?
Oscar?!
What if it doesn't work?
What do I do?
What now?

> *Long pause.*

Oscar, wait!
I'm coming.
I'm coming too.

THE END

D 505 THEATRE AND LA MAMA PRESENTS
E WORLD PREMIERE OF

ELL'S CANYON
Y EMILY SHEEHAN

ll's Canyon was first presented at The
d 505 Theatre on the 1st of August 2018
d transferred to La Mama Theatre on
e 12th of September 2018. The play
as developed with Playwriting Australia
the National Script Workshop and the
tional Play Festival. *Hell's Canyon* won
e Rodney Seaborn Playwrights Award
d was shortlisted for the Patrick White
aywrights Award.

rector Katie Cawthorne
signer Tyler Ray Hawkins
und Designer Kimmo Vennonen
age Manager Laura Barnes

st Isabelle Ford and Conor Leach

ver Photography Ellen Stanistreet
ver and Program Design Jen Tran

ACT Government · playwriting australia · LA MAMA

With the support and encouragement of many talented artists with much more experience than me, I began to write my first play, *Hell's Canyon*.

I wrote *Hell's Canyon* to try make sense of the grief and rage and pain I felt as a young person. When your world is falling apart it can feel impossible to hold onto any sense of optimism. It's only in the moments you realise who and what makes it all worth it, can you find the will to swim to the surface, even if all you want to do is sink.

For me, the heart of this play is contained within one of Caitlin's final lines, 'When you think your heart might break. Let it. It's hard for the world to get bigger when you're clinging to a piece that's about to break. So, let it break, and let it break open.'

This is a play about learning to break open.

Caitlin and Oscar are learning to create room within themselves. Space that's big enough to contain the immensity of what is going on for each of them. I think if we can find a way to create that room, we're able to contain what's happening, and include it as part of ourselves, without it becoming all of ourselves.

Thank you firstly to Jane Bodie who read it first and without whom I would have written a much worse play. Thank you also to the many artists who helped me develop the script along the way; the wonderful people at Playwriting Australia, as well as Isabelle Ford, Darcy Brown, Sarah Giles and Christie Evangelisto. Thank you to the Currency Press family, particularly Claire Grady, as well as The SBW Foundation and Arts ACT. And finally, thank you to Katie for your imagination and rigour, and to Izzy, Conor, Tyler, Kimmo and Laura who have filled the rehearsal room with so much creativity and generosity.

PLAYWRIGHT'S NOTES

Human nature is predictable no matter where we sit in history. No matter who we are, we all have times in our lives where the life we're living is difficult. Many of us have times that are more than difficult, they're truly challenging. And then some of us experience moments where life is actually gruelling. Caitlin is experiencing this at the age of seventeen. The secret she is keeping is beginning to pull her downwards and is much heavier than she anticipated. Oscar holds a secret too. At teen he has seen things adults wouldn't want to contemplate.

Emily Sheehan writes the young voice so honestly. And the young voice is one I believe we need to listen to more actively in our world. It has been such an intimate and intense process in the rehearsal room, as we've discovered the zest, humour and fear in this story, as well as the solace we can all find in drinking warm milo. This hard working and caring team of creatives have explored the psychologies of Caitlin and Oscar and the choices they've made, most importantly, without judgement.

Hell's Canyon is encouragement to swim to the surface, even if the life you're living feels too heavy to keep gripping on to.

DIRECTOR'S
NOTES

Emily Sheehan
Playwright

Katie Cawthorne
Director

Emily Sheehan is an award-winning playwright and theatre maker. Emily completed her Masters in Playwriting at the Victorian College of the Arts (VCA) in 2015 where she was awarded a creative scholarship, and her Bachelor of Arts (Acting) in 2011. Her first play *Hell's Canyon* won the Rodney Seaborn Playwrights Award, was shortlisted for the Patrick White Playwrights Award, and was a showcased play in Playwriting Australia's 2016 National Play Festival at The Malthouse Theatre. Her second play, *Daisy Moon Was Born This Way*, was commissioned and produced by The Joan as part of their 2017 season. Her third play, *versions of us*, was commissioned by Canberra Youth Theatre and performed at the Ralph Wilson Theatre in 2017. Emily has worked as a script assessor for Playwriting Australia, and as a dramaturgy intern with Melbourne Theatre Company. In 2014, Emily undertook a six-month traineeship in script assessment and new play development with Playwriting Australia. Emily is directing *Faster* at Canberra Youth Theatre in 2018, a new work co-devised with the cast.

Katie began directing in 2002 and ha presented work in Melbourne, Sydne Mexico, Darwin and Canberra. Kat completed her Masters of Fine Ar (Directing) at the National Institute Dramatic Arts (NIDA) in 2015. She ha been the Artistic Director of Canber Youth Theatre since January 201 For Canberra Youth Theatre Katie ha directed *SKIN*, *The 24 Hour Butc Project*, *The Verbatim Project*, *The Gree Project: Antigone*, *poem every day* ar *Filtered*. In 2016 Katie was awarded Canberra Critics' Circle Theatre Awar for 'Revitalising and Advancing Canber Youth Theatre'. Since graduating fro NIDA, Katie has also directed short worl for Warehouse Circus, The Public Theat (Design Canberra Festival) and Aspe Island Theatre Company. Katie is c founder of The Anchor theatre compan which produced its first show, *How A You?* at The Public Theatre in 2015. Th Anchor are currently developing a fu length version of *How Are You?* to l presented at Kings Cross Theatre in 201

CREATIVE
TEAM

abelle Ford
aitlin

Conor Leach
Oscar

1belle studied a Bachelor of Arts (Acting) Federation University Art Academy, d is a graduate of the 16th Street :tors Studio Program. Isabelle has ted in many short films, music videos, d television commercials. Her theatre edits include: *Daisy Moon Was Born This* ay (The Joan), *Hell's Canyon* (Playwriting istralia National Play Festival), *Aotearoa* ow (Playwriting Australia National Play stival), *Untold* (Melbourne Theatre ompany Cybec Electric), *Peer Gynt* ederation University), and *The Golden* ve (Federation University). Having ad the part of Caitlin in *Hell's Canyon* Playwriting Australia's National Play stival in 2016, Isabelle is ecstatic to be orising the role.

Conor is a Melbourne-based actor and theatre maker and a 2017 graduate of the Victorian College of the Arts (VCA) Bachelor of Fine Arts (Acting). Conor's theatre credits include: *Dancing with Death* (Arts Centre Melbourne / AsiaTOPA Festival), *AntigoneX* (Theatre Works), *NINETEEN NINETY-NINE* (Melbourne Fringe Festival). For VCA: *The Caucasian Chalk Circle* (dir. Michael Kantor), *Three Sisters* (dir. Melanie Beddie) and *The Wonderful World of Dissocia* (dir. Luke Kerridge). Conor was one of Australian Theatre for Young People's Fresh Ink playwrights, and has created works for Queensland Theatre and the Festival of Australian Student Theatre. He is also an accomplished vocalist and pianist. Screen credits include: *Sequin in a Blue Room* (dir. Samuel van Grinsven).

Kimmo Vennonen
Sound Designer

Kimmo Vennonen is a creative artist combining sound, music and electronics, specialising in sound design and CD mastering. From his Canberra studio he works with people and companies around Australia, frequently in music, dance and theatre. In 1991 he contributed as an improvising musician to the radio special *Collaborations* that won the Prix Italia for the ABC. In the 1990s he studied at the Australian National University with Greg Schiemer and David Worrall, specialising in immersive sound in a geodesic dome, leading to being an ANU Visiting Fellow 1995-1998. In 2010 he won the MEAA Green Room Award for "creative and innovative sound design". He currently convenes Sound Design and Production for the University of Canberra. Kimmo looks forward to more collaboration and exploration and approaches sound as a plastic art. Image courtesy of Peter Hislop.

Tyler Ray Hawkins
Designer

As a 2017 NIDA Masters of Fine Arts Design graduate, Tyler has already bee fortunate enough to work with Sydn Theatre Co., Opera Australia, Belvo Theatre, Griffin Theatre Co, ATY Romance was Born, Sass & Bide, Dollhou Pictures, and Underbelly Arts. Previo Theatre design work includes: *L.O.T.R.A* (Next Wave Festival 2018), *Greater Sunri* (Belvoir 25a), *Howling Girls* (Sydn Chamber Opera, Carriageworks), *Dolor* (SamProductions), *Intersection: Chrysa* (ATYP) *Wasted* (TKC, Factory Theat Marrickville), *Watermelon* (Underbelly A Festival 2017), *Moth* (ATYP), *A Strateg Plan* (Griffin Theatre), *Hanging Garde* *of Babylon* (Opera Australia), *Black Bir* (Black Birds, Joan Sutherland Performi Arts Centre), *A Midsummer Night's Drea* (Sydney Theatre Co), *The Wonderful Wiza* *of Oz* (Belvoir Theatre), *I Hate you M* *Mother* (Red Line Productions), *#KillAllMe* and *The Olympians* (NIDA), *Out of Gas c* *Lover's Leap*, *This is Our Youth*, *Grueson* *Playground Injuries* and *The Wonder* *World of Dissocia* (The Kings Collectiv Previous Screen Design work include *A Chance Affair* (Nobel Savage Picture *Brown Lips* (Nakkiah Lui, Noble Sava Pictures), *Saint Lo* (Nick Waterman, Meg Washington) and *Eaglehawk* (Shann Murphy, Dollhouse Collective). Prior his study at NIDA, Tyler graduated w a Bachelor of Fine Arts (Dance) at t Victorian College of the Arts in 2008. H has worked as a professional contempora dancer independently and for compani such as Chunky Move, Lucy Guerin Inc a Opera Australia.

CREATIVE TEAM

aura Barnes
age Manager

ura Barnes began taking part in ckstage work at the age of fifteen and s hardly moved from stage left since. e aspires to support theatre-makers in eating challenging and exciting works th interesting technical elements. orking predominately in independent eatre, her recent theatre credits include: *ida*, *Windows*, and *La Nonna* (La ama), *Everything is Fine* (Four Letter ord) and *Feed* (Ringtail Theatre). Laura is rrently studying a Bachelor of Fine Arts roduction) in stage management at the ctorian College of the Arts (VCA).

The *Hell's Canyon* team would like to thank the following:

Seaborn, Broughton & Walford Foundation

playwriting australia
Playwriting Australia

ACT Government
Arts ACT

THE UNIVERSITY OF MELBOURNE | **VCA** Victorian College of the Arts
Victorian College of the Arts

Old 505 Theatre

LA MAMA
La Mama Theatre

THANK YOU

The Old 505 Theatre is a creation of the artist-led and run company 505. Old 505 Theatre offers artists and actors a place to nurture new work, having built a solid reputation for our high caliber program, it offers local audiences a quality theatre experience. This underpins our ability to nurture a number of not-for-profits, artist-run associations, and independent performers, providing them a refreshing home where performance and creation of new work takes precedence. Importantly, it is a space from which these organisations and artists can publicise and promote their work to the wider community, and develop their artists' voice in a dedicated cultural facility. Our team is committed to offering a performance-focused theatre that is artist orientated. New Australian stories and devised work form the core of what we do.

In 2018, La Mama celebrated 51 years of nurturing new Australian Theatre.

Built in 1883 for Anthony Reuben Ford, a Carlton printer, the building in Faraday Street had been used as a workshop, a boot and shoe factory, an electrical engineering workshop and a silk underwear factory before becoming a theatre in 1967. It was established by Betty Burstall and modelled on experimental theatre activities in New York. Jack Hibberd's play *Three Old Friends* was the first play performed in the tiny space. Since that time the crowded intimacy of La Mama has provided welcome opportunities to a host of playwrights, actors, directors, technicians, filmmakers, poets and comedians, such as David Williamson, Barry Dickins, John Romeril, Tes Lyssiotis, Lloyd Jones, the Cantrills, Judith Lucy, Richard Frankland, Julia Zemiro, and Cate Blanchett … the list of those who have been nurtured there is long.

Unfortunately on Saturday the 19th of May 2018, La Mama Theatre was extensively damaged by fire caused by an electrical fault. A huge outpouring of love and support from the Carlton community, from many arts and non-arts organisations, from funding bodies, audience members, media, schools and La Mama's extensive community of artists is helping La Mama to move forward with optimism and energy. Planning has already begun to rebuild and restore La Mama for the next 50 years and beyond.

For updates and details on how to support the future of La Mama, go to: www.lamama.com.au

ABOUT OLD 505 THEATRE

ABOUT LA MAMA THEATRE